EXECUTIVE SUMMARY

Advances in emerging surveillance technologies like cell-site simulators – devices which transform a cell phone into a real-time tracking device – require careful evaluation to ensure their use is consistent with the protections afforded under the First and Fourth Amendments to the U.S. Constitution.

The United States' military and intelligence agencies have developed robust and sophisticated surveillance technologies for deployment in defense against threats from foreign actors. These technologies are essential to keeping America safe.

Increasingly though, domestic law enforcement at the federal, state, and local levels are using surveillance technologies in their every-day crime-fighting activities. In the case of cell-site simulators, this technology is being used to investigate a wide range of criminal activity, from human trafficking to narcotics trafficking, as well as kidnapping, and to assist in the apprehension of dangerous and violent fugitives.

Law enforcement officers at all levels perform an incredibly difficult and important job and deserve our thanks and appreciation. While law enforcement agencies should be able to utilize technology as a tool to help officers be safe and accomplish their missions, absent proper oversight and safeguards, the domestic use of cell-site simulators may well infringe upon the constitutional rights of citizens to be free from unreasonable searches and seizures, as well as the right to free association. Transparency and accountability are therefore critical to ensuring that when domestic law enforcement decide to use these devices on American citizens, the devices are used in a manner that meets the requirements and protections of the Constitution.

After press reports alleged wide-spread use of cell-site simulation devices by federal, state, and local law enforcement,[1] the Committee initiated a bipartisan investigation in April 2015.[2] At the outset of the investigation, the use of these devices by federal, state, and local law enforcement agencies was not well known, and in many instances, appeared to be shrouded in

---

[1] *See, e.g.*, Devlin Barrett, *Americans' Cellphones Targeted in Secret U.S. Spy Program*, WALL ST. J., Nov. 13, 2014, *available at* http://www.wsj.com/articles/americans-cellphones-targeted-in-secret-u-s-spy-program-1415917533; Kim Zetter, *The Feds Are Now Using 'Stingrays' in Planes to Spy on Our Phone Calls*, WIRED (Nov. 14, 2014, 2:14 PM), http://www.wired.com/2014/11/feds-motherfng-stingrays-motherfng-planes/.

[2] *See* Hon. Jason Chaffetz, et al., Chairman, H. Comm. on Oversight and Gov't Reform to Hon. Eric H. Holder, Att'y Gen., U.S. Dept. of Justice and Hon. Jeh C. Johnson, Sec'y, U.S. Dep't of Homeland Sec. (Apr. 24, 2015), *available at* https://oversight house.gov/wp-content/uploads/2015/05/2015-04-24-JEC-EEC-WH-RK-to-Johnson-DHS-stingrays-due-5-8.pdf; https://oversight house.gov/wp-content/uploads/2015/05/2015-04-24-JEC-EEC-WH-RK-to-Holder-DOJ-stingrays-due-5-8.pdf. The Committee's investigation was focused on domestic law enforcement use and intentionally did not examine use outside of the United States or in national security matters. The Committee received information from 24 federal agencies about their possession and use of cell-site simulation technology in the context of domestic surveillance; the Committee will conduct oversight over use of the technology in other contexts as warranted.

secrecy.[3] This is partly due to the use of the technology by military and intelligence agencies and the need for sensitivity in national security matters. The Federal Bureau of Investigation (FBI), for example, avoided disclosing not only its own use of the devices, but also its role in assisting state and local law enforcement agencies in obtaining and deploying these devices. Indeed, the Committee's investigation revealed that as part of the conditions for being able to sell cell-site simulators to state and local law enforcement, the manufacturers of these devices must first notify the FBI, and those agencies in turn must sign a non-disclosure agreement with the FBI that expressly prohibits them from publicly disclosing their use of this technology, even in prosecutions where the use of the technology was at issue.[4]

On April 24, 2015, the Committee sent letters to then-Attorney General Eric Holder and Homeland Security Director Jeh Johnson, requesting information about their agencies' use of cell-site simulators and the privacy concerns inherent with their use.[5]

Due to Possible Copyright Concerns,
Image has been Removed

Image: Courtesy of U.S. Patent and Trade Office[6]

---

[3] *See* Stephanie K. Pell & Christopher Soghoian, *Your Secret StingRay's No Secret Anymore: The Vanishing Government Monopoly Over Cell Phone Surveillance and its Impact on National Security and Consumer Privacy*, 28 HARV. J.L. & TECH. 1, 38 (2014).

[4] Briefing by Fed. Bureau of Investigation to H. Comm. on Oversight & Gov't Reform staff (Feb. 11, 2015); *see also* Letter from Ernest Reith, Acting Assistant Dir., Operational Tech. Div., Fed. Bureau of Investigation, to Frederick H. Bealefeld, III, Police Comm'r, Baltimore Police Dep't, et al. (July 13, 2011); Pell & Soghoian, supra note 3, at 38.

[5] Letters from Hon. Jason Chaffetz, et al., Chairman, H. Comm. on Oversight and Gov't Reform to Hon. Eric H. Holder, Att'y Gen., U.S. Dept. of Justice and Hon. Jeh C. Johnson, Sec'y, U.S. Dep't of Homeland Sec. (Apr. 24, 2015), *available at* https://oversight.house.gov/wp-content/uploads/2015/05/2015-04-24-JEC-EEC-WH-RK-to-Johnson-DHS-stingrays-due-5-8.pdf; https://oversight.house.gov/wp-content/uploads/2015/05/2015-04-24-JEC-EEC-WH-RK-to-Holder-DOJ-stingrays-due-5-8.pdf.

[6] The image is available here: http://www.ocregister.com/articles/stingray-653962-aclu-police.html.

During the course of the investigation, it became clear that the use of cell-site simulators by state and local law enforcement agencies was not governed by any uniform standards or policies. In an effort to determine how widespread this problem was, the Committee identified four cities of varying sizes and crime rates, along with two states, for the purpose of ascertaining the number and type of cell-site simulators in use, as well as the policies that were employed for their use. In particular, the Committee sent letters to the police departments in Washington, D.C.; Alexandria, Virginia; Sunrise, Florida; Baltimore, Maryland; the Tennessee Bureau of Investigation; and the Virginia State Police, requesting among other things, information regarding the number, the funding, and the use of these devices at the state and local level.

Documents and information obtained by the Committee confirmed varying standards for employing cell-site simulation devices among federal, state, and local law enforcement. Notably, the documents and information revealed that when the Committee first began its investigation in April 2015, federal law enforcement entities could obtain a court's authorization to use cell-site simulators by meeting a standard lower than probable cause — the standard to obtain a search warrant.

On October 21, 2015 the Committee's Subcommittee on Information Technology (the Subcommittee) held a public hearing on DOJ's and DHS's use of cell-site simulators.[7] The hearing focused on the agencies' policies and procedures for deploying cell-site simulation technology. In September 2015, five months into the Committee's investigation and with the hearing upcoming, DOJ announced a new policy for its use of cell-site simulation devices.[8] Shortly thereafter, DHS followed suit with the announcement of a similar new policy.

At the hearing, it became evident that prior to the Committee's investigation, the component law enforcement entities of DHS and DOJ had different policies and procedures governing their use of this technology and the agencies were not always obtaining a probable cause based warrant prior to deploying these devices. The new policies substantially changed how the agencies obtain authorization to deploy cell-site simulation technology. The new policies also introduced a measure of uniformity to how the various component agencies of each department used cell-site simulators, and importantly, required the agencies to obtain a warrant supported by probable cause in the majority of situations.

---

[7] *Hearing on Examining Law Enforcement Use of Cell Phone Tracking Devices* Before the H. Comm. on Oversight and Gov't Reform, Subcomm. on Info. Tech., 114th Cong. 69 (2015).

[8] U.S. Dep't of Justice, *Justice Department Announces Enhanced Policy for Use of Cell-Site Simulators* (Sept. 3, 2015), http://www.justice.gov/opa/pr/justice-department-announces-enhanced-policy-use-cell-site-simulators.

- The Department of Justice has <u>310 cell-site simulation devices</u> and spent <u>more than $71 million</u> in fiscal years 2010-14 on cell-site simulation technology.

- The Department of Homeland Security has <u>124 cell-site simulation devices</u> and spent <u>more than $24 million</u> in fiscal years 2010-14 on cell-site simulation technology.

- DHS allows state and local law enforcement to purchase cell-site simulation technology using grants from the Preparedness Grant Program administered by the Federal Emergency Management Agency (FEMA), including the State Homeland Security Program, Law Enforcement Terrorism Prevention Program, Citizen Corps Program, Urban Areas Security Initiative, Emergency Management Performance Grants, Buffer Zone Protection Program, Transit Security Program, and the Intercity Passenger Rail Program.

- DHS was able to identify <u>more than $1.8 million</u> in grant money to state and local law enforcement to purchase cell-site simulation technology, however DHS does not maintain a separate accounting of grant funds used to purchase cell site-simulators and the total amount may be higher.

- Before DOJ and DHS issued their new and enhanced policies for the use of cell-site simulators—which now require a warrant supported by probable cause—federal law enforcement agencies had varying policies and most relied on a lower-than-probable cause standard for use of these devices in most, but not all, situations.

- State laws continue to vary as to what court authorization is required before law enforcement can deploy cell-site simulators. Several states, including California,[9] Washington,[10] Virginia,[11] Utah,[12] and Illinois[13] have passed laws requiring law enforcement agencies to obtain a warrant or order based on probable cause before deploying cell-site simulators, with varying exceptions.

- In many cases, state and local law enforcement continue to rely on the state equivalent of a pen register/trap and trace order, which only requires law enforcement to meet a "relevance based standard" to use cell-site simulation devices, a standard lower than probable cause.

- Costs of individual cell-site simulator devices ranged from $41,500 to as high as $500,000.

---

[9] The California Electronic Communications Privacy Act, Cal. Penal Code § 1546 (2015).
[10] Wash. Rev. Code § 9.73.260 "Pen registers, trap and trace devices, cell site simulator devices" (2015).
[11] Va. Code §19.2-70.3 (2016).
[12] Utah Code § 77-23c-102 (2016).
[13] The Citizen Privacy Protection Act, 725 ILCS 137 (2016).

TABLE OF CONTENTS

Cell-site simulators are devices that effectively transform a cell phone into a real time tracking device. A cell-site simulator—also known as an "IMSI catcher"—is a device that mimics a cell phone tower.[14] These devices are commonly referred to as "Stingrays," which is both a generic name and also refers to a specific type of IMSI catcher that is manufactured by the Harris Corporation.[15] When the device is activated, cell phones in the surrounding area connect to the device in a similar way that the cell phones would connect to a cell tower. Once a phone connects to the cell-site simulator, the device is capable of obtaining specific identifying information for the phone, including information that enables law enforcement to determine the location of the phone and, more importantly, its user.[16] The devices were initially designed for the military, but were later adapted for domestic law enforcement. Law enforcement agencies usually operate them from moving vehicles or, to a lesser extent, from airplanes.[17]

Over the past five years, DOJ and DHS combined to spend approximately $95 million to acquire various types of cell-site simulators. Additionally, DHS has provided more than $1.8 million in grant money to state and local law enforcement to purchase cell-site simulators.[18]

In order to better understand the breadth of federal, state, and local law enforcement agencies' use of domestic cell-site simulation technology, the Committee met with each of the relevant component agencies of DOJ and DHS, the Internal Revenue Service (IRS), the Treasury Inspector General for Tax Administration (TIGTA), and the Department of Defense (DOD).[19] The Committee also obtained an in-person demonstration of this technology.[20]

Documents and information obtained by the Committee also confirmed reports of the widespread use of non-disclosure agreements that bound law enforcement not to reveal their use of these devices and even went so far as to require local prosecutors to agree to dismiss any of

---

[14] *See generally* Pell & Soghoian, *supra* note 3, at 11-12 (explaining how a cell-site simulator works).

[15] *See* Harris Corporation, Stingray Product Description (online at http://files.cloudprivacy net/Harris_Stingray_product_sheet.pdf) (last visited Nov. 15, 2016) (explaining that the "StingRay is Harris' latest offering in a long line of advanced wireless surveillance products.").

[16] *See, e.g.*, Pell & Soghoian, *supra* note 3, at 11-12, 17-19 (discussing how cell-site simulators work and the types of information the devices can obtain).

[17] *See, e.g.*, Barrett, *supra* note 1.

[18] *Hearing on Examining Law Enforcement Use of Cell Phone Tracking Devices* Before the H. Comm. on Oversight and Gov't Reform, Subcomm. on Info. Tech., 114th Cong. 69 (2015) (Responses to Questions for the Record Submitted to Seth Stodder, Assistant Sec'y, Threat Prevention and Sec. Policy, U.S. Dep't of Homeland Sec., by Hon. Jason Chaffetz, Chairman, H. Comm. on Oversight and Gov't Reform).

[19] Briefing by U.S. Dep't of Homeland Sec. to H. Comm. on Oversight & Gov't Reform staff (May 22, 2015); Briefing by U.S. Dep't of Justice to H. Comm. on Oversight & Gov't Reform staff and H. Comm. on Judiciary staff (Sept. 18, 2015); Briefing by Internal Revenue Serv. to H. Comm. on Oversight & Gov't Reform staff (Nov. 12, 2015); Briefing by Treasury Inspector Gen. for Tax Admin. to H. Comm. on Oversight & Gov't Reform staff (Jan. 20, 2016); Briefing by U.S. Dep't of Def. to H. Comm. on Oversight & Gov't Reform staff (May 4, 2016).

[20] Field demonstration of cell-site simulator technology by Bureau of Alcohol, Tobacco, Firearms and Explosives, to H. Comm. on Oversight & Gov't Reform staff (May 29, 2015).

their criminal cases if the FBI did not approve the disclosure of the devices in any particular case.[21]

From April to August 2015, Committee staff met with the component agencies and officials from DOJ and DHS leadership; from those meetings, two things became clear: (1) use of these devices was widespread; and (2) there was a lack of uniformity across the agencies regarding what court authority was required to deploy cell-site simulation technology under different operating scenarios.[22]

[Intentionally Left Blank]

---

[21] Briefing by Fed. Bureau of Investigation to H. Comm. on Oversight & Gov't Reform staff (May 13, 2015). For reports see Brad Heath, *Police Secretly Track Cellphones to Solve Routine Crimes*, USA TODAY, Aug. 24, 2015, *available at* http://www.usatoday.com/story/news/2015/08/23/baltimore-police-stingray-cell-surveillance/31994181/; *see also* Jemal R. Brinson, *Data: Cell Site Simulators: How Law Enforcement Can Track You,* CHI. TRIB., Feb. 18, 2016, *available at* http://www.chicagotribune.com/news/plus/ct-cellphone-tracking-devices-20160129-htmlstory html.
[22] *See supra* note 19.

Cell phones are designed to seek out and connect to the strongest cell phone tower they can find in their vicinity.[23] Cell-site simulators work by impersonating a cell phone tower. Cell phones within range recognize the device as the strongest cell phone tower in the area and connect with the device.[24] Every cell phone has a unique identifying number assigned by a device manufacturer or a cellular network provider called the International Mobile Subscriber Identity (IMSI).[25] When the cell-site simulator connects with a cell phone, the simulator is able to identify that cell phone's unique identifying number.[26] In addition, most cell-site simulators have the ability to collect and store the IMSI numbers of all the phones they connect with in the area where they are deployed.[27]

[Intentionally Left Blank]

---

[23] *See* Brinson, *supra* note 21.

[24] U.S. Dep't of Justice, *Department of Justice Policy Guidance: Use of Cell-Site Stimulator Technology* at 2 [*hereinafter DOJ Cell Site Policy*], http://www.justice.gov/opa/file/767321/download (discussing how cell-site simulators function).

[25] *See id.*; Brinson, *supra* note 21.

[26] *DOJ Cell Site Policy*, *supra* note 24, at 2.

[27] *See* Pell & Soghoian, *supra* note 3, at 11-12.

Due to Possible Copyright Concerns,
Image has been Removed

Image: USA Today[28]

An IMSI catcher is an example of an active surveillance device. It "exploit[s] the lack of authentication of the base station by cellular phones," and "[a]s a result, phones have no way to differentiate between a legitimate base station owned or operated by the target's wireless carrier and a rogue device impersonating a carrier's base station."[29] Most current phones—those on 3G and 4G networks—"now include the capability for phones to authenticate the network base stations," but even these current models "are backward compatible with older, vulnerable phone network technologies, which allows the phone to function if it is taken to a rural location or foreign country where the only service offered is 2G."[30]

In addition to vehicle-based use of the devices, some law enforcement agencies mount the devices on planes.[31] Airborne use covers a wider geographic range, and when deployed over populated areas, a significantly higher number of phones with no connection to criminal activity are surveilled.

---

[28] Image: *Cell Data Investigation: How We Did It*, USA TODAY, (June 10, 2014),
http://www.usatoday.com/story/news/nation/2013/12/08/cellphone-data-investigation-how/3902857/.
[29] Pell & Soghoian, *supra* note 3, at 12.
[30] *Id.* at 12 n.52.
[31] Barrett, *supra* note 1.

Due to Possible Copyright Concerns,
Image has been Removed

Image: Wall Street Journal[32]

The Committee obtained information from federal, state, and local law enforcement that shows the majority of situations where a cell-site simulator is deployed involve the search for a specific, known cell phone.[33] In this scenario, law enforcement first obtains the target cell phone's number through traditional investigative methods. Once the target cell phone number is ascertained, law enforcement generally obtains the IMSI number that is associated with that cell phone number from the cellular service provider. A warrant is generally not a prerequisite to requesting the IMSI number from the service provider; in many instances, law enforcement obtains the IMSI number by issuing an administrative subpoena to a cell phone service provider.[34]

After obtaining the IMSI number, the simulator is deployed in search of the phone. When the device is brought within the range of that specific cell phone, the device will stop connecting with other cell phones in the area and lock in on that particular phone. The device

---

[32] Image: *Id.*

[33] Briefing by U.S. Immigration Customs and Enforcement to H. Comm. on Oversight & Gov't Reform staff (Feb. 3, 2015); Briefing by Fed. Bureau of Investigation to H. Comm. on Oversight & Gov't Reform staff (Feb. 11, 2015); Briefings by U.S. Marshals Serv. to H. Comm. on Oversight & Gov't Reform staff (Mar. 25 and 31, 2015); Briefing by U.S. Drug Enforcement Admin. to H. Comm. on Oversight & Gov't Reform staff (Apr. 7, 2015); Briefings by U.S. Dep't of Homeland Sec. to H. Comm. on Oversight & Gov't Reform staff (May 7, 11, and 22, 2015); Briefing by Bureau of Alcohol, Tobacco, Firearms and Explosives to H. Comm. on Oversight & Gov't Reform staff (May 21, 2015); Briefing by Baltimore Police Dep't to H. Comm. on Oversight & Gov't Reform staff (June 30, 2015); Field demonstration of cell-site simulator technology by Bureau of Alcohol, Tobacco, Firearms and Explosives to H. Comm. on Oversight & Gov't Reform staff (May 29, 2015).

[34] *See generally supra* note 33.

then receives signals from the cell phone that provide information indicating whether the device is moving closer to or farther away from the targeted cell phone. Law enforcement then uses this information to narrow the location of the phone down to a specific area where law enforcement can conduct a search for the phone and presumably, the person carrying it.[35]

While the devices are frequently used to track down fugitives and other known, wanted targets, they can also be used as an investigative tool. When deployed in this fashion, the device can be used to identify the IMSI number during the course of an investigation, and the IMSI numbers of any individuals who are present with the target.[36]

To use the device as an investigative tool, law enforcement deploys the device at a known location of the target and obtains every IMSI number in the vicinity at the time of deployment. By deploying the device numerous times in numerous locations where the targeted individual is present, law enforcement collects a list of IMSI numbers for each cell phone present at every location where the device was deployed. The device analyzes this list to determine if there were common IMSI numbers at each location. By a process of elimination, the common IMSI numbers are identified as likely to be those of the target's phone, and individuals associated with the target. Law enforcement can then work with cellular service providers to determine telephone numbers and billing information associated with specific IMSI numbers.[37]

Likewise, the devices could be deployed at groups of people who assemble at different times in different places to eventually determine the identities of individuals whose IMSI numbers become associated with that group. When used as an investigative tool, the device stores the identifying numbers for a limited period of time to analyze them for the purpose of distinguishing the targeted device(s).[38]

Whenever a cell-site simulator is deployed, there are collateral consequences for the non-target phones in the area. While searching for the target phone, the simulator will also make contact with other, non-target cell phones that happen to be within range of the simulator device, even if those phones' owners are innocent bystanders who are not suspected of any criminal wrongdoing. The simulator identifies and collects these non-target phones' unique identifiers as well. When searching for a specific IMSI number, the device identifies and drops contact with the non-targeted phones within a few seconds.[39]

In testimony before the Committee, DOJ and DHS both confirmed the simulator devices they use do not intercept any communications or content from the cellular devices to which they connect. Specifically, DOJ confirmed that between January 1, 2010 and September 2, 2015, its

---

[35] *See supra* note 33.

[36] *See, e.g.*, Jennifer Valentino-Devries, *How 'Stingray' Devices Work*, WALL ST. J. (Sept. 21, 2013, 10:33 PM), http://blogs.wsj.com/digits/2011/09/21/how-stingray-devices-work/; Brinson, *supra* note 21.

[37] *See supra* note 33.

[38] Briefing by Fed. Bureau of Investigation to H. Comm. on Oversight & Gov't Reform staff (Feb. 11, 2015); Briefing by U.S. Marshals Serv. to H. Comm. on Oversight & Gov't Reform staff (Mar. 25, 2015); Briefing by U.S. Dep't of Homeland Sec. to H. Comm. on Oversight & Gov't Reform staff (May 7, 11, and 22, 2015).

[39] *See* Pell & Soghoian, *supra* note 3, at 12 (discussing how when used, cell-site simulators and similar surveillance technology "also pick up the signals of other phones used by innocent third parties."); *supra* note 33.

component agencies using the technology—the FBI; the Drug Enforcement Administration (DEA); the Bureau of Alcohol, Tobacco, Firearms and Explosives (ATF); and U.S. Marshals Service (USMS)—only collected dialing, routing, signaling and addressing information in domestic criminal investigations and did not use the devices to collect the content of communications.[40] While the current DOJ and DHS policies require the cell-site simulators to be configured as pen registers and to not collect content, some of the cell-site simulator models used by law enforcement components within DOJ and DHS would be capable of collecting content if the devices had the necessary software installed.[41]

FEDERAL LAW ENFORCEMENT'S ACQUISITION AND POSSESSION OF CELL-SITE SIMULATORS

The Committee obtained documents and information that showed the quantity, make and model, and cost of cell-site simulators purchased by DOJ and DHS for fiscal years 2010-14. The documents and information revealed the following:

In fiscal years 2010-2014, DOJ spent more than $71 million to acquire and use cell-site simulation technology. Costs of individual devices ranged from $41,500 to as high as $460,000. The spending by component agency breaks down as follows: [42]

- Drug Enforcement Administration (DEA) – approximately $7,000,000
- U.S. Marshals Service (USMS) – approximately $12,500,000
- Bureau of Alcohol, Tobacco and Firearms (ATF) – approximately $15,000,000
- Federal Bureau of Investigation (FBI) – approximately $35,000,000

DOJ has 310 devices agency-wide. The total number of devices in possession of each agency component is broken down as follows:

- DEA – 33
- USMS – 70
- ATF – 13
- FBI – 194

[40] *Hearing on Examining Law Enforcement Use of Cell Phone Tracking Devices* Before the H. Comm. on Oversight and Gov't Reform, Subcomm. on Info. Tech., 114th Cong. 69 (2015) (Response of Elana Tyrangiel, Principal Deputy Assistant Att'y Gen. of the United States Response 1 to Questions for the Record) (Copy on file with the Committee).

[41] *Hearing on Examining Law Enforcement Use of Cell Phone Tracking Devices* Before the H. Comm. on Oversight and Gov't Reform, Subcomm. on Info. Tech., 114th Cong. 69 (2015) (Response of Elana Tyrangiel, Principal Deputy Assistant Att'y Gen. of the United States Response 1, 2 and 4 to Questions for the Record) (Copy on file with the Committee).

[42] Briefings by U.S. Dep't of Justice to H. Comm. on Oversight & Gov't Reform staff (June 26, 2015, July 1 and 24, 2015).

In fiscal years 2010-2014, DHS spent more than $24 million to acquire and use cell-site simulation technology. Costs of individual devices ranged from $93,000 to as high as $500,000. The spending by component agency breaks down as follows:[43]

- Immigration and Customs Enforcement (ICE) – approximately $10,500,000
- United States Secret Service (USSS) – approximately $10,500,000
- Customs and Border Patrol (CBP) – approximately $2,500,000

DHS has 124 devices agency-wide. The total number of devices in possession of each agency component is broken down as follows:

- ICE – 59
- USSS – 32
- CBP – 33

The Committee also obtained documents and information that showed the quantity, make and model, and cost of cell-site simulators purchased by the Treasury Department (Treasury) since January, 2006. The information and documents showed as follows:

Since January 2006, Treasury has spent more than $1.3 million to acquire and use cell-site simulation technology. The spending by component agency breaks down as follows:[44]

- IRS Criminal Investigations – approximately $1,040,586
- Treasury Inspector General – approximately $260,000

Treasury has a total of 3 devices agency-wide. The total number of devices in possession of each agency component is as follows:[45]

- IRS Criminal Investigations – 2
- Treasury Inspector General – 1

---

[43] Briefing by Bureau of Alcohol, Tobacco, Firearms and Explosives to H. Comm. on Oversight & Gov't Reform staff (May 21, 2015); Briefing by U.S. Dep't of Homeland Sec. to H. Comm. on Oversight & Gov't Reform staff (May 22, 2015).

[44] Letter from Hon. John Koskinen, Comm'r, Internal Revenue Serv., Dep't of the Treasury, to Hon. Jason Chaffetz, Chairman and Hon. Elijah E. Cummings, Ranking Member, H. Comm. on Oversight and Gov't Reform (Nov. 17, 2015); Letter from Timothy P. Camus, Deputy Inspector Gen. for Investigations, Inspector Gen. for Tax Admin., to Hon. Jason Chaffetz, Chairman and Hon. Elijah E. Cummings, Ranking Member, H. Comm. on Oversight and Gov't Reform (Jan. 13, 2016).

[45] Letter from Hon. John Koskinen, Comm'r, Internal Revenue Serv., Dep't of the Treasury, to Hon. Jason Chaffetz, Chairman and Hon. Elijah E. Cummings, Ranking Member, H. Comm. on Oversight and Gov't Reform (Nov. 17, 2015); Letter from Timothy P. Camus, Deputy Inspector Gen. for Investigations, Inspector Gen. for Tax Admin. to Hon. Jason Chaffetz, Chairman and Hon. Elijah E. Cummings, Ranking Member, H. Comm. on Oversight and Gov't Reform (Jan. 13, 2016).

The Supreme Court in recent years has decided a number of cases that clarify citizens' Fourth Amendment protections in the digital age.[46] At the federal level, DOJ has instituted several policies to govern how it uses technology to track people, its most recent being a new and enhanced policy on how its agencies use cell-site simulators.[47] In addition to DOJ, DHS has adopted a similar new policy.[48]

Cell-Site Simulators and the Fourth Amendment

As devices capable of tracking individuals have developed over time, the courts have been tasked with determining whether the Fourth Amendment's protections apply to an individual's movements. In evaluating Fourth Amendment protections, the court considers whether or not a person has a subjective expectation of privacy in the area being viewed and whether society is prepared to deem that expectation reasonable.[49]

In two cases from the 1980s, the Supreme Court decided cases involving devices being used to track objects from place to place. In *United States v. Knotts*,[50] law enforcement placed a tracking beeper inside a container that a narcotics suspect then placed into his car. Police subsequently began to conduct visual surveillance on the suspect with the assistance of the beeper. The visual surveillance eventually ended when the suspect undertook evasive maneuvers, however, law enforcement was still able to track the container the suspect was carrying by tracking the beeper's signals, which ultimately led them to a cabin the suspect was occupying.[51] The issue before the Court was whether a warrantless monitoring of the beeper violated the Fourth Amendment. The Court ruled that the beeper signals did not invade any legitimate expectation of privacy on the suspect's part, and therefore, concluded that "there was neither a 'search' nor a 'seizure' within the contemplation of the Fourth Amendment."[52] In reaching its conclusion, the Court found that the beeper surveillance amounted principally to following an automobile on public streets, and under the Court's analysis, the mere fact that law enforcement had used a beeper device to enhance their ability to conduct visual surveillance in a

---

[46] Under the Fourth Amendment to the U.S. Constitution, citizens are afforded the following protections: "The right of the people to be secure in their persons, houses, papers, and effects, against unreasonable searches and seizures, shall not be violated, and no warrants shall issue, but upon probable cause, supported by Oath or affirmation, and particularly describing the place to be searched, and the persons or things to be seized." U.S. CONST. amend. IV.

[47] U.S. Dep't of Justice, *Justice Department Announces Enhanced Policy for Use of Cell-Site Simulators* (Sept. 3, 2015), https://www.justice.gov/opa/pr/justice-department-announces-enhanced-policy-use-cell-site-simulators.

[48] U.S. Dep't of Homeland Sec., *DHS Policy Regarding The Use of Cell-Site Simulator Technology* (Oct. 21, 2015), https://www.dhs.gov/publication/dhs-policy-regarding-use-cell-site-simulator-technology.

[49] Katz v. United States, 389 U.S. 347, 361 (1967) (Harlan, J., concurring).

[50] 460 U.S. 276 (1983).

[51] *See id.* at 277-79.

[52] *Id.* at 285.

public place did not turn that surveillance into a search that was prohibited by the Fourth Amendment.[53]

One year after *Knotts*, the Court decided *United States v. Karo*,[54] a case in which law enforcement agents had again placed a tracking beeper inside a container without first obtaining a warrant. In *Karo*, law enforcement agents obtained location information by monitoring the device as the container was moved around among two private residences and a storage facility.[55] The Court concluded that absent a search warrant, "the monitoring of a beeper in a private residence, a location not open to visual surveillance, violates the Fourth Amendment rights of those who have a justifiable interest in the privacy of the residence."[56] In issuing its ruling, the Court explicitly warned that "[i]ndiscriminate [electronic] monitoring of property that has been withdrawn from public view would present far too serious a threat to privacy interests in the home to escape entirely some sort of Fourth Amendment oversight."[57]

In 2012, the Court issued its decision in *United States v. Jones*,[58] which concerned the issue of "whether the attachment of a Global-Positioning-System (GPS) tracking device to an individual's vehicle, and subsequent use of that device to monitor the vehicle's movements on public streets, constitutes a search or seizure within the meaning of the Fourth Amendment."[59] The Court unanimously ruled that the government's installation of a GPS tracking device on a vehicle and tracking of that vehicle's movements for four weeks constituted a search under the Fourth Amendment.[60] In *Jones*, FBI agents had placed a GPS tracker on a suspect's car while the car was parked on private property. The agents then monitored the vehicle's location for approximately one month. The FBI, however, did not properly obtain a warrant prior to placing the GPS device on the car nor did it do so during the subsequent monitoring of the car's location throughout the State of Maryland.[61]

While the *Jones* decision was unanimous, the justices differed on what specific law enforcement activity had violated the Fourth Amendment. The majority of the Court held that the attachment of the device onto the vehicle was a trespass by law enforcement onto private property and that law enforcement's attempt to obtain information from that trespass constituted an illegal search.[62] Justice Alito, in a concurring opinion, argued that the length of time law enforcement spent tracking the defendant's vehicle made this a violation of the defendant's reasonable expectation of privacy under the Fourth Amendment.[63] Justice Sotomayor, in a concurring opinion, found that both the trespass and the length of the monitoring constituted a

---

[53] *Id.* at 281-83.
[54] 468 U.S. 705 (1984).
[55] *See id.* at 708-11.
[56] *Id.* at 714.
[57] *Id.* at. 716.
[58] 565 U.S. 400 (2012).
[59] *Id.* at 402.
[60] *Id.* at 403-04.
[61] *See id.* at 402-03.
[62] *Id.* at 404-12.
[63] U.S. v. Jones, 565 U.S. at 429-31 (2012).

search under the Fourth Amendment and questioned whether individuals lose all privacy protections when they provide information such as computer transmissions to a third party.[64]

Although *Jones* now makes clear that the police must obtain a warrant before placing a GPS device on a person's property, the decision did not address all forms of warrantless tracking law enforcement may engage in. For example, the Court's decision did not address cases where the police obtain geolocation information from a person's cellphone or car without having to physically attach a device to track its movements, such as in the case of electronic devices that are already outfitted with GPS tracking technologies.[65]

THE *JONES* MEMOS

In light of the evolving landscape of the Supreme Court's Fourth Amendment case law, and its application in the digital age, the Committee was interested in learning how DOJ interpreted the tracking requirements the Court set out in *Jones*.

DOJ created guidance following the Jones decision

At a February 2012 University of San Francisco Law Review Symposium, then-FBI General Counsel Andrew Weissmann revealed that in light of the Court's *Jones* decision, DOJ had generated two memoranda to be provided to its component agencies: 1) guidance to the field specifically on the use of GPS; and 2) guidance on what *Jones* means for other types of geolocation techniques beyond GPS (hereinafter, "the *Jones* Memos").[66]

When the Committee began its investigation of domestic law enforcement's use of cell-site simulation technology, the only publicly available information on the actual contents of the *Jones* Memos, aside from Mr. Weissmann's comments, were two heavily redacted Guidance memoranda DOJ had released in response to a Freedom of Information Act request from the American Civil Liberties Union.[67]

As part of the Committee's investigation, DOJ agreed to produce the *Jones* Memos for an *in camera* review by this Committee.[68] Consistent with that agreement, on April 14, 2016,

---

[64] *Id.* at 413-18.

[65] Richard M. Thompson II, CONG. RESEARCH SERV., R42511: *UNITED STATES V. JONES:* GPS MONITORING, PROPERTY, AND PRIVACY, (2012).

[66] 2012 University of San Francisco Law Review Symposium, *Big Brother in the 21st Century? Reforming the Electronic Communications Privacy Act*, YOUTUBE (Feb. 29, 2012), https://www.youtube.com/watch?v=C5f6VDUbGXs.

[67] The redacted memos provided to ACLU can be found on the ACLU's website at https://www.aclu.org/files/assets/doj_gps_tracking_memo1.pdf and https://www.aclu.org/files/assets/doj_post-jones_tracking_memo1.pdf.

[68] Email from Eric P. Losick, Office of Legislative Affairs, U.S. Dep't of Justice, to H. Comm. on Oversight and Gov't Reform staff (Mar. 1, 2016).

Chairman Chaffetz and Ranking Member Cummings, along with Committee staff, reviewed *in camera* the *Jones* Memos. These two memorandums are briefly discussed below.[69]

The first memorandum begins with a review of the *Jones* case and includes the basic facts, the holding, and an overview of the majority opinion, as well as the concurring opinions. As part of the Committee's investigation, DOJ shared examples of briefs in which its prosecutors had argued that the accessing of historical cell-site information was not a search under the Fourth Amendment. DOJ also provided examples of cases in which it had argued that agents, acting prior to the *Jones* decision, had operated under the good faith exception to the Fourth Amendment, which allows law enforcement to still use materials that were obtained in a search a court determines was improper if law enforcement relied in good faith upon case law as it existed at the time of the search. DOJ has also testified that "in light of the *Jones* decision, law enforcement agents now generally obtain a search warrant supported by probable cause before the installation and monitoring of a tracking device on a vehicle. There are, however, circumstances including long-standing exceptions to the warrant requirement, such as consent or exigent circumstances, where a warrant would not be required."[70] The Committee's investigation indicated that these positions had been taken consistent with the memorandum.

The second memorandum examines the application of *Jones* to non-GPS geolocation tracking techniques, including, but not limited to, historical cell-site records, security cameras mounted on street poles and private businesses, automatic license plate readers, transit records such as E-Z pass and metro cards, and cell-site simulators. The second memorandum focused on the extent to which the Court's reliance on a physical trespass theory in *Jones* would require law enforcement to obtain a probable cause warrant in circumstances that did not involve a physical trespass.

DOJ'S PRIOR POLICIES PERTAINING TO GEOLOCATION

Prior to the Committee's investigation into cell-site simulators, DOJ and its component agencies were using geolocation technologies under a less rigid set of guidelines for ensuring that citizens' Fourth Amendment rights were adequately protected. Those guidelines, which are set forth below, were inadequate to protect the privacy interests of American citizens who found themselves within range of an active cell-site simulator.

---

[69] Since DOJ would only agree to voluntarily produce these documents for an *in camera* review, the complete unredacted versions of these documents remain in the possession of the agency.

[70] *Hearing on Geolocation Technology and Privacy* Before the H. Comm. on Oversight and Gov't Reform., 114th Cong. (Mar. 2, 2016) (Written Testimony, Richard Downing, Deputy Assistant Att'y Gen. (Acting), U.S. Dep't of Justice).

Pen Register Statute

When the Committee begin its oversight of law enforcement's use of cell-site simulators, DOJ and its component agencies did not have to obtain a warrant based on probable cause. DOJ instead had generally obtained court authorization to use cell-site simulators by seeking an order under the Pen Register and Trap and Trace Statute ("The Pen Register Statute").[71] The Pen Register Statute establishes a framework by which the government can receive court authorization to obtain non-content information about outgoing and incoming phone calls. The Pen Register Statute governs law enforcement's ability to obtain the specific telephone numbers of incoming and outgoing calls for a particular phone through the use of pen register and trap and trace devices. A "pen register" is a device which records the numbers a phone dials out, whereas a "trap and trace device" records the specific telephone numbers of incoming calls.[72] While court authorization for pen registers and trap and trace devices is required, this authorization takes the form of an order, rather than a warrant.

To obtain an order to deploy pen registers and trap and trace devices, the Pen Register Statute requires the government to establish that the information likely to be obtained by the pen register or trap and trace device is *relevant* to an ongoing criminal investigation.[73] In *Smith v. Maryland*,[74] the Court concluded that individuals do not have an expectation of privacy in the numbers dialed to and from a home telephone because "a person has no legitimate expectation of privacy in information he voluntarily turns over to third parties."[75] As such, to date, installation and use of a pen register to record the numbers dialed from a specific telephone is not subject to the Fourth Amendment's more stringent warrant requirement. Rather, the use of a pen register is subject only to the legislative requirement of a court order that is based solely on the government's demonstration that the information may be relevant to an ongoing investigation. The relevance standard is less of a burden than the probable cause standard for search warrants, and it is far lower than the burden that law enforcement is required to meet to obtain and make use of a wiretap.[76]

The first public judicial opinion dealing with a request by law enforcement to use a cell-site simulator came in 2012 from a federal magistrate judge in Texas.[77] In that case, the government sought to use a "pen register and trap and trace device . . . to detect radio signals emit[ing] from wireless cellular telephones in the vicinity of the [subject] that identify the telephones (e.g., by transmitting the telephone's serial number and phone number) to the network for authentication."[78] In support of its application, the government asserted that doing so would permit it to identify the telephone number being used by the subject of the investigation. In an *ex*

---

[71] *See generally* 18 U.S.C. §§ 3121-3127; *supra* note 33.

[72] *Id.* at § 3127.

[73] *Id.* at § 3123.

[74] 442 U.S. 735 (1979).

[75] *Id.* at 743-44.

[76] 18 U.S.C. § 2518.

[77] *In re* Application of the United States of America for an Order Authorizing the Installation and Use of a Pen Register and Trap and Trace Device, 890 F. Supp. 2d 747 (S.D. Tex. 2012).

[78] *Id.* at 748 (internal quotations omitted); *see also* Pell & Soghoian, *supra* note 3, at 28-29.

parte hearing with the magistrate judge, the special agent leading the investigation testified that he intended to use a cell-site simulator to identify the cell phone numbers.[79]

The magistrate judge ultimately denied the application to use the cell-site simulator on the ground that the application failed to explain how the device worked and would be used to "engage in electronic surveillance,"[80] the distance the device needed to be located from the subject, and what the "government would do with the cell phone numbers and other information concerning seemingly innocent cell phone users whose information was recorded by the equipment."[81]

Pre-2015 Cell-Site Simulator Guidance

DOJ's policy on what court authorization the agency would obtain prior to deploying cell-site simulators has changed over the years, most recently, just prior to the October 2015 Subcommittee hearing on the devices. A 1997 DOJ guidance bulletin discussed the agency's views on what legal authority governed the various law enforcement surveillance options, including "cell-site simulator."[82] According to the 1997 guidance, DOJ took the position that "it does not appear that there are constitutional or statutory constraints on the warrantless use of such a device."[83] According to a chart that was issued with the guidance, court orders, search warrants, and subpoena requirements were not applicable when deploying this device.[84]

While DOJ believed that these devices could be deployed without obtaining any prior authorization from any court, the DOJ policy was that if the devices were "used as pen registers or trap and trace devices, they should be used pursuant to a court order issued pursuant to these statutes."[85] Other than to note in the chart that legal process was not applicable to use of these devices for cell-site locale information, the guidance did not expand on the use of these devices to determine a cell phone's "cell-site locale."[86]

The 2001 PATRIOT Act amended the Pen Register Statute and added the term "signaling information" to the definition of information that required court authorization before law enforcement could intercept it.[87]

---

[79] 890 F. Supp. 2d at 748.
[80] *Id.* at 749-52.
[81] *Id.*
[82] U.S. Dep't of Justice, *Electronic Surveillance Techniques,* "Electronic Surveillance Guide" p. 14, Vol. 45, No. 5, Sept. 1997, *available at* https://www.justice.gov/sites/default/files/usao/legacy/2007/01/11/usab4505.pdf.
[83] *Id.* at 18.
[84] *Id.*
[85] *Id.* at 14.
[86] *Id.* at 18.
[87] 18 U.S.C. § 3127(3).

The 2005 version of DOJ's Electronic Surveillance Manual contains a section on "Cell Site Simulators / Digital Analyzers / Triggerfish."[88] The 2005 guidance advises United States Attorneys:

> Because section 3127 of Title 18 defines pen registers and trap and trace devices in terms of recording, decoding or capturing dialing, routing, addressing, or signaling information, a pen register/trap and trace order must be obtained by the government before it can use its own device to capture the ESN or MIN of a cellular telephone, even though there will be no involvement by the service provider.[89]

During the course of the Committee's investigation, it became clear the FBI was drawing a distinction between deploying cell-site simulators on targets in public places and deploying the devices to collect information when a person was in a private space, such as a home. If the device were to be deployed to detect a person when they were believed to be in their home, the FBI would obtain a warrant. When an individual was believed to be on a street or some other public space, however, the FBI relied upon an order under the Pen Register Statute.[90]

DOJ's Policy Requires a Warrant for use of a Cell-Site Simulator

On September 3, 2015 DOJ announced its most recent, enhanced policy for use of cell-site simulators.[91] This policy now governs each of its component agencies use of these devices. DOJ's new policy requires its component agencies to obtain a search warrant supported by probable cause and issued pursuant to Rule 41 of the Federal Rules of Criminal Procedure or the applicable state equivalent, with some limited exceptions.[92]

The DOJ policy makes clear that not only is a warrant required for use of cell-site simulators, but that the warrant must meet certain cell-site simulator-specific requirements. Warrant applications must include sufficient information to ensure that courts are aware that it is an application to use cell-site simulator technology, and affirm that law enforcement will make no affirmative investigative use of any non-target data absent further order of the court.[93] The warrant application must also disclose that there may be ancillary service disruption to non-target phones.[94]

DOJ's policy also makes clear that the use of cell-site simulation devices will be disclosed to defendants in accordance with long-standing discovery rules. The policy states:

---

[88] Electronic Surveillance Manual Procedures and Case Law Forms, U.S. Dep't of Justice, https://www.justice.gov/sites/default/files/criminal/legacy/2014/10/29/elec-sur-manual.pdf (last updated June 2005).
[89] Id.
[90] Briefings by U.S. Dep't of Justice and Fed. Bureau of Investigation to H. Comm. on Oversight & Gov't Reform staff (Feb. 11, 2015, May 13, 2015).
[91] U.S. Dep't of Justice, *Justice Department Announces Enhanced Policy for Use of Cell-Site Simulators* (Sept. 3, 2015), https://www.justice.gov/opa/pr/justice-department-announces-enhanced-policy-use-cell-site-simulators.
[92] *DOJ Cell Site Policy, supra* note 24, at 3.
[93] *Id.* at 5.
[94] *Id.*

As in any criminal prosecution, the Department will abide by the Federal Rules of Criminal Procedure, including Rule 16, as well as any pertinent authority governing disclosures to the defendant, including the assertion of the law enforcement sensitive qualified evidentiary privilege where appropriate to protect sensitive information about the operation of the device. The Department's policy emphasizes the need to comply with all legal disclosure requirements and for candor to the court in legal filings related to such devices.[95]

The DOJ policy also addresses the issue of data collection and disposal. When a device is used to locate a known phone, any data retrieved by the device while searching for that phone must be deleted as soon as the known phone is located, and no less than once daily.[96] When a device is used to identify a target phone, the data on the device must be deleted no less than every 30 days.[97]

Emergency, or so-called exigent, circumstances have long provided an exception to the Fourth Amendment's requirement to obtain a search warrant. The DOJ's policy references several exigent circumstances that allow law enforcement to proceed without a warrant including "the need to protect human life or avert serious injury" and the "hot pursuit of a fleeing felon."[98] In these exigent circumstances situations, DOJ policy still requires the use of the device to comply with the Pen Register Statute.[99] DOJ expects instances where this exception applies to be "very limited" and will require approval from executive level personnel at the agency's headquarters, the relevant U.S. Attorney, and from a Criminal Division Deputy Assistant Attorney General.[100]

DOJ's policy also creates an exception to the warrant requirement for exceptional circumstances where the law does not require a search warrant and circumstances make obtaining a search warrant impracticable.[101] In briefings with Committee staff, DOJ stated that this is an amorphous category that is not expected to arise frequently.[102] As with the exigent circumstances exception, the use of a simulator under this exception still must comply with the Pen Register Statute.[103] DOJ has indicated it intends to keep statistics about the number of occasions the devices are used without a warrant pursuant to both of these exceptions.

---

[95] *Hearing on Examining Law Enforcement Use of Cell Phone Tracking Devices* Before the H. Comm. on Oversight and Gov't Reform, Subcomm. on Info. Tech., 114th Cong. 69 (2015) (Response of Elana Tyrangiel, Principal Deputy Assistant Att'y Gen. of the United States Response 5 to Questions for the Record).

[96] *DOJ Cell Site Policy, supra* note 24, at 6.

[97] *Id.*

[98] *Id.* at 3. It should be noted that simply being a fugitive wanted by the United States Marshals Service (USMS) will not merit an exigent circumstances exception to the warrant requirement.

[99] *Id.* at 4.

[100] *Id.*

[101] *Id.*

[102] Briefing by U.S. Dep't of Justice to H. Comm. on Oversight & Gov't Reform and H. Comm. on Judiciary staff (Sept. 18, 2015).

[103] *Id.*

DHS Follows DOJ's Lead in Requiring a Warrant to use a Cell-Site Simulator

On October 19, 2015, DHS issued its policy for the use of the devices.[104] It is substantially similar to DOJ's policy. Like the DOJ policy, DHS's policy requires that: the devices be configured as pen registers (that is, not to capture content);[105] DHS component agencies are to obtain a search warrant grounded in probable cause before using the devices;[106] that non-warrant use must fall within the exigent or exceptional circumstances (and then the agents must still comply with the Pen Register Statute);[107] agents must notify the court that the devices will be used and the potential effect on non-target phones;[108] and agents are to delete the data from the devices no less frequently than once every 30 days.[109]

However, unlike the DOJ policy, DHS's policy permits "[a]ffected DHS Components" to "issue additional specific guidance consistent with this policy."[110] In addition, each affected DHS component agency was to designate a point of contact for implementation of the policy by mid-November, 2015.[111] Additionally, unlike DOJ's policy, DHS's policy does not require the agency to keep statistics for cases of non-warrant use.

ADDITIONAL FEDERAL AGENCIES' USE OF CELL-SITE SIMULATION TECHNOLOGY

In addition to the law enforcement component agencies contained within DOJ and DHS, the Committee also investigated whether other agencies within the federal government were deploying cell-site simulation technology in a domestic enforcement capacity. The Committee sent letters to 24 federal agencies inquiring about their possession and use of these devices.

In response to those letters, the Internal Revenue Service (IRS) and the Treasury Inspector General for Tax Administration (TIGTA) both indicated that they own cell-site simulators.[112]

---

[104] U.S. Dep't of Homeland Sec., *Department Policy Regarding the Use of Cell-Site Simulator Technology* (Oct. 19, 2015), https://www.dhs.gov/sites/default/files/publications/Department%20Policy%20Regarding%20the%20Use%20of%20Cell-Site%20Simulator%20Technology.pdf. This policy was issued two days before the Subcommittee on Information Technology held a hearing on the issue.

[105] *Id.* at 3.

[106] *Id.* at 4 (noting that agents will, "[a]s a practical matter . . . seek authority pursuant to" the rule pertaining to search warrants, as well as "the Pen Register Statute").

[107] *Id.* at 4-5.

[108] *Id.* at 6.

[109] *Id.* at 6.

[110] *Id.* at 2.

[111] *Id.* at 3.

[112] Letter from Hon. John Koskinen, Comm'r, Internal Revenue Serv., Dep't of the Treasury, to Hon. Jason Chaffetz, Chairman and Hon. Elijah E. Cummings, Ranking Member, H. Comm. on Oversight and Gov't Reform (Nov. 17, 2015); Letter from Timothy P. Camus, Deputy Inspector Gen. for Investigations, Inspector Gen. for Tax Admin. to Hon. Jason Chaffetz, Chairman and Hon. Elijah E. Cummings, Ranking Member, H. Comm. on Oversight and Gov't Reform (Jan. 13, 2016).

Media reports in August, 2015 disclosed that the IRS possesses cell-site simulation technology.[113] On October 29, 2015, the Committee sent a letter to the IRS requesting information on the IRS's possession and use of cell-site simulators.[114] The agency's November 17, 2015 response to that letter confirmed that the IRS did in fact possess cell-site simulators.[115] Since January 2006, the IRS has purchased two cell-site simulators at a cost of more than $900,000. In response to a series of questions to an IRS witness during a hearing on April 13, 2016, the IRS subsequently notified the Committee that the cell-site simulators it possesses are not capable of being reconfigured to collect content such as calls, text messages, pictures, or messaging through apps.[116]

According to the IRS, its first cell-site simulator was acquired in October 2011, and a second one was acquired in December 2015.[117] As of April 22, 2016, the IRS reported that since January 2006, it used cell-site simulators to track cellular devices as part of 37 federal IRS Criminal Investigation (CI) investigations.[118] In addition to their own tax code-related investigations, the IRS reported using cell-site simulators to assist in four non-IRS CI investigations—one federal investigation with the DEA and three state cases.[119]

More specifically, the IRS CI used the technology to pursue cases involving money laundering, identity theft, and a single case of "structuring" that the United States Attorney's Office declined to prosecute.[120] The majority of the federal cases involved money laundering related to drug trafficking.[121]

---

[113] Nicky Woolf & William Green, *IRS Possessed Stingray Cellphone Surveillance Gear, Documents Reveal*, THE GUARDIAN, Oct. 26, 2015, *available at* http://www.theguardian.com/world/2015/oct/26/stingray-surveillance-technology-irs-cellphone-tower.

[114] Letters from Hon. Jason Chaffetz, et al., Chairman, H. Comm. on Oversight and Gov't Reform, to Hon. John Koskinen, Comm'r, Internal Revenue Serv. (October 29, 2015) *available at*: https://oversight house.gov/wp-content/uploads/2015/10/2015-10-29-JC-EEC-WH-RK-to-Koskinen-IRS-Stingray-due-11-12-resp-11-6-briefing.pdf.

[115] Letter from Letter from Hon. John Koskinen, Comm'r, Internal Revenue Serv., Dep't of the Treasury, to Hon. Jason Chaffetz, Chairman and Hon. Elijah E. Cummings, Ranking Member, H. Comm. on Oversight and Gov't Reform (Nov. 17, 2015).

[116] *Hearing on Waste and Inefficiency in the Federal Government: GAO's 2016 Duplication Report* Before the H. Comm. on Oversight & Gov't Reform, 114th Cong. (Apr. 13, 2016) (IRS written responses to Committee Questions for the Record on file with the Committee).

[117] *Id.*; Letter from Hon. John Koskinen, Comm'r, Internal Revenue Serv., Dep't of the Treasury, to Hon. Jason Chaffetz, Chairman and Hon. Elijah E. Cummings, Ranking Member, H. Comm. on Oversight and Gov't Reform (Nov. 17, 2015).

[118] Letter from the Dep't of the Treasury, Internal Revenue Serv., to Hon. Jason Chaffetz, Chairman and Hon. Elijah E. Cummings, Ranking Member, H. Comm. on Oversight and Gov't Reform (Apr. 22, 2016).

[119] *Id.*

[120] *Hearing on Waste and Inefficiency in the Federal Government: GAO's 2016 Duplication Report* Before the H. Comm. on Oversight & Gov't Reform, 114th Cong. (Apr. 13, 2016) (Statement of Mr. John Dalrymple, Deputy Commissioner, Services and Enforcement, Internal Revenue Serv., in Responses to Hearing Questions for the Record) (Aug. 30, 2016).

[121] *Id.*

In 2012, the IRS CI used cell-site simulators in a state/local case involving illegal firearms distribution and illegal possession of a firearm.[122] In 2015, IRS CI assisted state and local police departments with an investigation into a case alleging attempted murder, assault, and weapons possession. In another 2015 case, IRS CI agents assisted in a homicide investigation.[123]

For each of the 37 investigations that the IRS reported using a cell-site simulator, the agency reported that it worked with an Assistant United States Attorney or State Prosecutor, and obtained "an order or a warrant" based on a finding of probable cause in 36 instances. On one occasion out of the 37, the IRS obtained authorization to deploy a cell-site simulator by obtaining an order pursuant to the Pen Register Statute.[124] Ten of the federal cases resulted in indictments. Indictments were obtained in every instance where the IRS assisted a state or local police department's investigation.[125]

The IRS's response indicated that prior to the Committee's oversight of this issue, the agency did not have an express agency-wide policy that governed the use of cell-site simulation devices.[126] Instead, for the use of such technology, the IRS had been applying only the general guidelines that it had been using "for the use of pen registers and trap-and-trace devices, that is, technology used by cell-site simulators."[127] The IRS' response also indicated that with the exception of certain memoranda of understanding that it had executed with state/local law enforcement, it did "not have policies, guidance or memoranda on the use of cell-site simulation technology in conjunction with joint law enforcement operations at the state or local level."[128]

In November 2015, the IRS issued a memorandum setting forth its own policy for the use of cell-site simulators.[129] A footnote to that memorandum states that "this policy is not intended to create or confer any rights, privileges, or benefits on any person. It is not intended to have the force of law."[130] According to the policy, while the IRS had previously obtained authorization to use a cell-site simulator by seeking an order pursuant to the Pen Register Statute, the policy going forward would be to "obtain a search warrant supported by probable cause and issued pursuant to Rule 41 of the Federal Rules of Criminal Procedure."[131] As a practical matter, the policy advises obtaining a warrant that contains all the required information under the Pen Register Statute, or to seek a warrant and a pen register order concurrently.[132] Similar to the

---

[122] *Id.*

[123] *Id.*

[124] *Id.*

[125] *Id.*

[126] Letter from Hon. John Koskinen, Comm'r, Internal Revenue Serv., Dep't of the Treasury, to Hon. Jason Chaffetz, Chairman and Hon. Elijah E. Cummings, Ranking Member, H. Comm. on Oversight and Gov't Reform (Nov. 17, 2015).

[127] *Id.*

[128] *Id.*

[129] Memorandum for Special Agents in Charge, *Policy Regarding the Use of Cell-Site Simulator Technology*, from Richard Weber, Chief, Criminal Investigation; Dep't of the Treasury, Internal Revenue Serv.; (Nov. 30, 2015). (Copy on file with the Committee).

[130] *Id.* at 1 n.1.

[131] *Id.* at 3.

[132] *Id.* at 3-4.

DOJ and DHS policies, the new IRS policy does contain an "exigent circumstances" exception to obtaining a warrant.

The new IRS policy for deploying a cell-site simulator requires that law enforcement "disclose appropriately and accurately the underlying purpose and activities for which an order or authorization is sought."[133] This information must now include the general terms by which the device is to be employed, that other phones in the area, as well as the targeted phone might experience a temporary disruption of service, and inform the court about how law enforcement will address the deletion of the data collected.[134] The new policy also calls for the application to "indicate that law enforcement will make no affirmative investigation of any non-target data acquired absent further order of the court."[135] The new policy further calls for deleting all data from the cell-site simulator after the targeted device has been located and not less than once daily.[136] The new policy also mandates that before deploying the cell-site simulator for any other mission, the IRS operator must verify that the device has been cleared of any previous operational data.[137]

Inspector General for Tax Administration

The Committee sent letters to twenty-four federal agencies inquiring as to whether they or their inspectors general possess cell-site simulators. TIGTA was the only inspector general that reported owning these devices. TIGTA purchased one cell-site simulator in 2008 at the cost of $108,000.[138] TIGTA did not deploy the device for years; when TIGTA eventually did have an opportunity to deploy the device, TIGTA technicians realized that the device's software was out of date. The agency relied instead on equipment provided by the U.S. Secret Service.[139] TIGTA then upgraded the device's software at a cost of $151,421.[140] TIGTA has not deployed the device since it was upgraded.[141]

In response to the Committee's oversight, TIGTA has amended its cell-site simulator policy to include language requiring TIGTA agents to, before deploying a cell-site simulator, "first determine the feasibility of using the services of partner Federal Law Enforcement

---

[133] *Id.* at 4.

[134] *Id.* at 5.

[135] Memorandum for Special Agents in Charge, *Policy Regarding the Use of Cell-Site Simulator Technology* at 5, from Richard Weber, Chief, Criminal Investigation; Dep't of the Treasury, Internal Revenue Serv.; (Nov. 30, 2015). (Copy on file with the Committee).

[136] *Id.* at 6.

[137] *Id.*

[138] Letter from Timothy P. Camus, Deputy Inspector Gen. for Investigations, Inspector Gen. for Tax Admin., to Hon. Jason Chaffetz, Chairman and Hon. Elijah E. Cummings, Ranking Member, H. Comm. on Oversight and Gov't Reform (Jan. 13, 2016).

[139] Briefing by Treasury Inspector Gen. to H. Comm. on Oversight & Gov't Reform staff (Jan. 20, 2016).

[140] *Id.*

[141] *Id.*

agencies that use the technology on a regular basis."[142] TIGTA has also agreed to not obtain additional equipment or software upgrades for its current device.

Given the amount of money spent, the fact that no other IG owns a device, and the device has not been used, TIGTA should strongly consider decommissioning the device it has and agree to not acquire any cell-site simulators in the future.

STATE AND LOCAL LAW ENFORCEMENT USE OF CELL-SITE SIMULATORS

The Committee investigated several state and local law enforcement jurisdictions and their use and possession of these devices. In an attempt to gauge just how widespread and prolific these devices are, the Committee identified four cities of varying sizes and crime rates, and two states to ascertain the number and type of cell-site simulators in use as well as the policies employed. As explained more fully below, the Committee's investigation revealed that of the state and local jurisdictions it identified, they generally owned one or two cell-site simulators.

State and Local Law Enforcement Obtain Cell-Site Simulators

Cell-site simulators have been purchased by a wide variety of state and local jurisdictions. While some jurisdictions have purchased these devices with local funds, other jurisdictions have used federal grant money to purchase the devices. DHS allows the purchase of cell-site simulators through certain preparedness grant programs that are administered by FEMA.[143] FEMA policy specifically states that use of such equipment is subject to the prohibitions contained in Title III of the Omnibus Crime and Control and Safe Streets Act of 1968, 18 U.S.C. §§ 2510-2522.[144] Additionally, all grant recipients are required to execute a term and condition of their awards, including assured compliance with all applicable federal laws, executive orders, and regulations. DHS reports that while not specific to cell-site simulators, "the scope of these assurances prohibits grantee conduct that violates the Fourth Amendment or any provision of the Constitution of the United States and all other applicable federal laws."[145]

DOJ reported that it "generally does not provide cell-site simulators to State and local law enforcement or fund their purchase."[146] According to the Department, there are only a "handful

---

[142] Letter from Timothy P. Camus, Deputy Inspector Gen. for Investigations, Inspector General for Tax Admin., to, H. Comm. on Oversight and Gov't Reform staff (Dec. 13, 2016).

[143] *Hearing on Examining Law Enforcement Use of Cell Phone Tracking Devices* Before the H. Comm. on Oversight and Gov't Reform, Subcomm. on Info. Tech., 114th Cong. 69 (2015) (Responses to Questions for the Record Submitted to Seth Stodder, Assistant Sec'y, Threat Prevention and Sec. Policy, U.S. Dep't of Homeland Sec., by Hon. Jason Chaffetz, Chairman, H. Comm. on Oversight and Gov't Reform (May 25, 2016).

[144] *Id.*

[145] *Id.*

[146] *Hearing on Examining Law Enforcement Use of Cell Phone Tracking Devices* Before the H. Comm. on Oversight and Gov't Reform, Subcomm. on Info. Tech., 114th Cong. 69 (2015) (Statement of Elana Tyrangiel, Principal Deputy Assistant Att'y Gen. of the United States in Responses to Post Hearing Questions for the Record).

of instances" where DOJ grant money has been used to purchase cell-site simulators.[147] The Department has stated that it is "open to considering" whether federal grant recipients should be required to comply with its policy regarding the use of cell-site simulation technology.[148]

Although DOJ reported that it generally does not provide cell-site simulators to state or local law enforcement, in at least one instance, it did report that in October 2010, an FBI field office in North Carolina requested and received from FBI headquarters a cell-site simulator for loan to the North Carolina Bureau of Investigation for an "indeterminate period of time."[149] The FBI field office ultimately retrieved the loaned device and returned it to FBI headquarters.[150]

Cell-Site Simulator Policies at the State and Local Level

During the course of the Committee's investigation into federal agencies' use of cell-site simulators, it became concerned that such use by state and local law enforcement agencies was not governed by any uniform standards. The Committee sent requests to the police departments in Washington, D.C.; Alexandria, Virginia; Sunrise, Florida; Baltimore, Maryland; the Tennessee Bureau of Investigation; and the Virginia State Police. The Committee obtained information about the number and cost of the devices, the ways in which purchases were funded, and the court authorizations obtained before deploying the devices.

Numbers and Funding Sources

With respect to the number of devices and funding sources at these police departments, the Committee found as follows:

Department	Number of Devices	Funding Source
Washington D.C. Metropolitan Police[151]	One	Local[152]
City of Alexandria, Virginia[153]	One	Local
City of Sunrise, Florida[154]	Two	Local

---

[147] *Id.*

[148] *Id.*

[149] *Id.*

[150] *Id.*

[151] Letter from Cathy Lanier, Chief of Police, Metro. Police Dep't, Washington D.C. to Hon. Jason Chaffetz, Chairman and Hon. Elijah E. Cummings, Ranking Member, H. Comm. on Oversight and Gov't Reform (July 1, 2016).

[152] Washington D.C. Metro. Police Dep't has previously used DHS grant funds to purchase cell-site simulator technology. The current device was purchased with local funds. Briefing by Washington D.C. Metro. Police Dep't to H. Comm. on Oversight and Gov't Reform staff (Oct. 26, 2016).

[153] Letter from Earl L. Cook, Chief of Police, Alexandria Police Dep't, Alexandria VA to Hon. Jason Chaffetz, Chairman and Hon. Elijah E. Cummings, Ranking Member, H. Comm. on Oversight and Gov't Reform (July 1, 2016).

[154] Letter from Samuel I. Zeskind, Partner, Weiss Seerota Helfman Cole & Bierman on behalf of John E. Brooks, Chief of Police, Sunrise Florida to Hon. Jason Chaffetz, Chairman and Hon. Elijah E. Cummings, Ranking Member, H. Comm. on Oversight and Gov't Reform (July 14, 2016).

Baltimore Police Department[155]	Three (one in current use)	DHS grant
Tennessee Bureau of Investigation[156]	One	DHS grant
Virginia State Police[157]	Two (one in current use)	Local

Legal Standards

The responses to the Committee's letters to state and local agencies show the variation of the use of these devices at the state and local level.

The Baltimore Police Department provided a "Standard Operating Procedure" manual that governs its use of cell-site simulators (Baltimore Police Policy).[158] Under the Baltimore Police Policy, officers "are required to obtain tracking/search warrants for all violent crimes where a cell phone is involved."[159] There is an exception for exigent circumstances "when a tracking order/search warrants order cannot be obtained due to the incident happening after normal courtroom hours."[160]

The Tennessee Bureau of Investigation requires law enforcement to obtain a search warrant prior to operating a cell-site simulator with limited exceptions, to include when the owner of the device gives consent, and exigent circumstances.[161] One notable exception is if the user has posted his or her location within the last 24 hours on a social media website.[162]

The City of Alexandria, Virginia and the Virginia State Police both have written policies that require law enforcement to follow the requirements of Virginia state law, which specifically outlines court authorizations for cell-site simulators.[163]

The local prosecuting office in the District of Columbia is the United States Attorney's Office and, as such, Washington D.C. follows the DOJ policy governing the use of cell-site simulators.[164]

---

[155] Emails from Andrew G. Vetter, Dir. of Gov't Affairs, Baltimore Police Dep't to H. Comm. on Oversight and Gov't Reform Staff (July 1, 2016; Aug. 1, 2016).

[156] Letter from Janet Kleinfalter, Deputy Att'y Gen., State of Tennessee to Hon. Jason Chaffetz, Chairman and Hon. Elijah E. Cummings, Ranking Member, H. Comm. on Oversight and Gov't Reform (July 1, 2016).

[157] Letter from Col. W.S. (Steve) Flaherty to Hon. Jason Chaffetz, Chairman and Hon. Elijah E. Cummings, Ranking Member, H. Comm. on Oversight and Gov't Reform (July 8, 2016).

[158] Baltimore Police Dep't, *Standard Operating Procedure for: Advance Tactical Team*, June 9, 2016 (Copy on file with the Committee).

[159] *Id.*

[160] *Id.*

[161] Tennessee Bureau of Investigation, *Standard Operating Procedures Technical Services Unit* (Copy on file with the Committee).

[162] *Id.*

[163] Letter from Col. W.S. (Steve) Flaherty to Hon. Jason Chaffetz, Chairman and Hon. Elijah E. Cummings, Ranking Member, H. Comm. on Oversight and Gov't Reform (July 8, 2016).

[164] Letter from Cathy Lanier, Chief of Police, Metro. Police Dep't, Washington D.C. to Hon. Jason Chaffetz, Chairman and Hon. Elijah E. Cummings, Ranking Member, H. Comm. on Oversight and Gov't Reform (July 1, 2016).

The City of Sunrise, Florida indicated in its response that it also follows DOJ's policy on use of cell-site simulator technology. It is unclear what the policy was prior to DOJ issuing its new and enhanced policy.[165]

State law varies in its treatment of cell-site simulators. Several states, including California,[166] Washington,[167] Virginia,[168] Utah,[169] and Illinois[170] have passed laws requiring law enforcement agencies to obtain a warrant before deploying cell-site simulators. In addition to these state legislative requirements, state courts have begun ruling on cases where police deployed cell-site simulators in their investigations. The Supreme Court of Florida has ruled that law enforcement must obtain a warrant based on probable cause prior to using a cell-site simulator to obtain a person's location information.[171] Likewise, in a recent opinion, an appellate court in Maryland reached a similar conclusion.[172] Specifically, the court there found:

> [P]eople have a reasonable expectation that their cell phones will not be used as real-time tracking devices by law enforcement, and – recognizing that the Fourth Amendment protects people and not simply areas – that people have an objectively reasonable expectation of privacy in real-time cell phone location information. Thus, we hold that the use of a cell site simulator requires a valid search warrant, or an order satisfying the constitutional requisites of a warrant, unless an established exception to the warrant requirement applies.[173]

In a separate Maryland case, a Baltimore judge reportedly suppressed crucial evidence in a murder case involving a "likely guilty" suspect after police deployed a cell-site simulator after obtaining a pen register order rather than a probable cause based search warrant.[174]

The lack of uniformity at the state and local level currently creates the possibility that states and localities are deploying cell-site simulator technology in a manner that is less strict than the guidelines being adhered to by federal law enforcement agencies. Insofar as state and local law enforcement receive federal grants to purchase these devices, DHS has acknowledged

---

[165] Letter from Samuel I. Zeskind, Partner, Weiss Seerota Helfman Cole & Bierman on behalf of John E. Brooks, Chief of Police, Sunrise Florida to Hon. Jason Chaffetz, Chairman and Hon. Elijah E. Cummings, Ranking Member, H. Comm. on Oversight and Gov't Reform (July 14, 2016).

[166] The California Electronic Communications Privacy Act, Cal. Penal Code § 1546 (2015).

[167] Wash. Rev. Code § 9.73.260 "Pen registers, trap and trace devices, cell site simulator devices (2015).

[168] Va. Code §19.2-70.3 (2016).

[169] Utah Code § 77-23c-102 (2016).

[170] The Citizen Privacy Protection Act, 725 ILCS 137 (2016).

[171] Tracey v. Florida, 152 So. 3d 504 (Fla. 2014) (suppressing evidence obtained from a warrantless use of an IMSI catcher).

[172] Maryland v. Andrews, 134 A.3d 324 (Md. Ct. Spec. App. 2016).

[173] *Id.* at 355.

[174] Cyrus Farivar, *Judge Rules in Favor of "Likely Guilty" Murder Suspect Found via Stingray*, Ars Technica (Apr. 26, 2016), http://arstechnica.com/tech-policy/2016/04/citing-unconstitutional-search-via-stingray-judge-suppresses-murder-evidence/.

the need for potential improvements in the grant-making process to encourage recipients to adopt the more stringent federal guidelines for use of these devices. As DHS explained:

> DHS acknowledges that policies for use and training for law enforcement personnel who seek to acquire cell-cite simulator technology through FEMA's preparedness grant programs could further safeguard privacy and civil liberties protections. DHS will further examine whether grantee adoption of baseline policy provisions, including training requirements, should be mandated as a condition of purchase through FEMA's preparedness grant programs, and if so, how any necessary training can most effectively be delivered.[175]

Non-Disclosure Agreements

The Committee's investigation found that those state and local entities that do purchase a cell-site simulator frequently sign non-disclosure agreements with two entities, the company selling the device, and the FBI. In addition to the publicly available versions of the non-disclosure agreements,[176] the Committee also obtained copies of non-disclosure agreements between the FBI and various state and local jurisdictions. As explained more fully below, these non-disclosure agreements actively prohibit the public from learning about the use or role that a cell-site simulator may play in a state or local criminal investigation.

Because cell-site simulators operate over the airwaves, manufacturers of these devices must obtain a special license from the FCC to sell them.[177] As part of its condition of approving any sale, the FBI imposed a requirement on state and local entities that in order to obtain the devices, they must sign a non-disclosure agreement with the FBI.[178]

These non-disclosure agreements impose significant secrecy requirements on the state and local entities seeking to obtain cell-site simulators. A review of these agreements showed that all contained similar language that prohibited state and local entities from disclosing any information about their use of cell-site simulators. For example, the typical non-disclosure agreement required that for any state or local law enforcement entity looking to purchase the device, that entity would agree to "not, in any civil or criminal proceeding, use or provide any

---

[175] *Hearing on Examining Law Enforcement Use of Cell Phone Tracking Devices* Before the H. Comm. on Oversight and Gov't Reform, Subcomm. on Info. Tech., 114th Cong. 69 (2015) (Responses to Questions for the Record Submitted to Seth Stodder, Assistant Sec'y, Threat Prevention and Sec. Policy, U.S. Dep't of Homeland Sec., by Hon. Jason Chaffetz, Chairman, H. Comm. on Oversight and Gov't Reform (May 25, 2016).

[176] Stingray Nondisclosure Agreement, New York Civil Liberties Union, http://www nyclu.org/files/20120629-renondisclsure-obligations%28Harris-ECSO%29.pdf.

[177] *See, e.g.,* Brinson, *supra* note 21(explaining the role of nondisclosure agreements in connection with the sale of cell-site simulators); Pell & Soghoian, *supra* note 3, at 37-38 (discussing how FCC applications for the manufacture of cell-site simulators impose specific conditions on manufacturers).

[178] Briefing by Fed. Bureau of Investigation to H. Comm. on Oversight & Gov't Reform staff (May 13, 2015); *see also* Pell & Soghoian, *supra* note 3, at 37-38.

information concerning . . . wireless collection equipment/technology, its associated software, ..."[179]

These agreements condition the possession and use of cell-site simulators on an agreement by state or local law enforcement to dismiss a criminal case at the FBI's request rather than produce information that could compromise the devices. The following is an example of the type of language used in this regard:

> In addition, the [local law enforcement and prosecuting office] will, at the request of the FBI, seek dismissal of the case in lieu of using or providing, or allowing others to use or provide, any information concerning the Harris Corporation wireless collection equipment/technology, its associated software, operating manuals, and any related documentation (beyond the evidentiary results obtained through the use of the equipment/technology), if using or providing such information would potentially or actually compromise the equipment/technology.[180]

Numerous press reports discuss cases in which the non-disclosure agreement played a factor in the prosecution of suspected criminals. In Baltimore, for example, prosecutors reportedly withdrew evidence instead of disclosing the possible use of a cell-site simulator.[181] In St. Louis, prosecutors reportedly dropped robbery charges against three co-defendants rather than have an officer from the police intelligence unit testify about the use of a cell-site simulator device in the case.[182] In Erie County, New York, police reportedly used the device 47 times since 2010, but only once sought a court order to do so.[183] The updated DOJ policy does not discuss the FBI non-disclosure agreements.

Purchase Agreements with Manufacturers of the Devices

In addition to non-disclosure agreements signed with the FBI, state and local entities also sign purchase agreements with manufacturers that include non-disclosure requirements. These purchase agreements include general language that the buyer would obtain all necessary court orders and comply with all constitutional, federal, state, and local privacy laws. They also included language asserting that certain technical information about the technology was confidential and exempt from requests made under the Freedom of Information Act (FOIA).[184]

---

[179] Excerpt of Fed. Bureau of Investigation non-disclosure agreement on file with the Committee.
[180] *Id.*
[181] Justin Fenton, *Former High Court Judge: Stingray Secrecy 'Wrong,'* BALTIMORE SUN, Apr. 16, 2015, *available at* http://www.baltimoresun.com/news/maryland/crime/blog/bs-md-ci-stingray-murphy-react-20150415-story html.
[182] Robert Patrick, *St. Charles Woman Withdraws Guilty Plea in Case Linked to Secret FBI Cellphone Tracker*, ST. LOUIS POST-DISPATCH, Apr. 27, 2015, *available at* http://www.stltoday.com/news/local/crime-and-courts/stingray-defendant-allowed-to-withdraw-her-guilty-plea/article_70d5ae28-e819-59d8-a391-78fdd4602d9f html.
[183] Kim Zetter, *NY Cops Used 'Stingray' Spy Tool 46 Times Without Warrant*, WIRED (Apr. 7, 2015 5:08 PM), http://www.wired.com/2015/04/ny-cops-used-stingray-spy-tool-46-times-without-warrant/.
[184] Document on file with the Committee.

One of the manufacturers included in its terms and conditions of a sale language that the purchaser "shall not disclose, distribute, or disseminate any information regarding Customer's purchaser or use of" the equipment "to the public in any manner, including but not limited to: in press releases, in court documents and/or proceedings, internet or during other public forums or proceedings."[185] Additionally, as part of the condition of the sale, the manufacturer required that the purchaser "shall not in any civil or criminal proceeding, use or provide information concerning" the equipment or software "beyond the evidentiary results obtained through the use of Equipment and/or Software without the prior written consent" of the manufacturer.[186]

NON-LAW ENFORCEMENT USE AND PRIVACY

Cell-site simulator use inside the United States raises far-reaching issues concerning the use, extent, and legality of government surveillance authority. While the Committee's investigation and hearing focused on law enforcement's use of these devices, non-law enforcement and/or foreign government use of cell-site simulation technology also raises serious concerns.

Law enforcement agencies are not the only groups who may use cell-site simulation technology. It is possible, if not likely, bad actors will use these devices to further their aims. Criminals and spies, however, will not be adopting the DOJ and DHS policies and procedures or any other ethics of surveillance. They will not be self-limiting in their use of these devices so as to not capture the content of others' conversations. Criminals could use these devices to track potential victims or even members of law enforcement. One can imagine scenarios where criminals or foreign agents use this type of technology to intercept text messages and voice calls of law enforcement, corporate CEOs, or elected officials.

Congress and other government agencies must remain vigilant to ensure any use of cell-site simulation technology is within the bounds of the law. These devices have the potential to obtain content from cell phones—at this point in time, law enforcement chooses not to use the devices to collect content in domestic investigations. Other actors possessing similar devices would not be constrained by either the Constitution or choices and policies made by domestic law enforcement agencies.

While law enforcement in the United States has worked for years to keep its use of the device shrouded in secrecy, the outside world has been making, advertising, and discussing cell-site simulators for years.[187] One security consultant was able to outfit his automobile with a "do-it-yourself" surveillance equipment, which included a cell-site simulator.[188] IMEI and IMSI catchers appear for sale on the internet website Alibaba, a Chinese eBay-type online commerce

---

[185] *Id.*

[186] *Id.*

[187] Bruce Schneier, *The Further Democratization of Stingray*, SCHNEIER ON SECURITY, (Apr. 27, 2015 6:27 AM), https://www.schneier.com/blog/archives/2015/04/the_further_dem_1.html.

[188] Thomas Fox-Brewster, *Build Your Own Scary Surveillance Jeep for Under $5000 With This Hacker's Guide*, FORBES (Sep. 15, 2015), *available at* http://www.forbes.com/sites/thomasbrewster/2015/09/15/diy-stingray-jeep/#5f3b09f756bc.

site.[189] The Alibaba advertisements and descriptions for use of these devices indicate advanced capabilities as well as suggestions for aggressive use of the devices by law enforcement. The ads even suggest where the devices may be used:

> Fixed indoor: public places such as cybercafes, banks/ATM, hospitals, ticket offices, etc. They are deployed where people have to wait or stay.
>
> …
>
> Portable mode: it is convenient for plainclothes police to carry with them to follow, search and make detection at airports, hotels, stations, streets, nearby apartments, etc.[190]

Anyone found using cell-site simulator technology to either spy for a foreign government or to identify targets for a terrorist attack could be prosecuted under laws governing espionage by domestic or foreign agents or the anti-terrorism laws. When asked about any non-law enforcement and non-military use of cell-site simulators, DOJ provided the following response:

> The Department is aware of media reports alleging that "hobbyists" may be building and testing cell-site simulators. In addition, the Department is aware of isolated incidents in which a cell-site simulator may have been used by a private entity. Any such use of a cell-site simulator could be inconsistent with Federal law. *See* 18 U.S.C. §§ 2512, 3121.[191]

DHS informed the Committee that it has no knowledge of private use of cell-site simulators.[192]

The Wiretap Act portion of the Electronic Communications and Privacy Act makes it a federal crime to intercept private communications without consent. Violations of the prohibition on interception are punishable by fines and incarceration for up to five years.[193] Title 18, Section 3121 of the U.S. Code creates a general prohibition on pen register and trap and trace device use

---

[189] Bruce Schneier, *The Further Democratization of Stingray*, SCHNEIER ON SECURITY, (Apr. 27, 2015 6:27 AM), https://www.schneier.com/blog/archives/2015/04/the_further_dem_1.html; *see also* Nigeria New Security System Mobile Phone Catcher IMEI and IMSI, Alibaba, https://www.alibaba.com/product-detail/Nigeria-New-Security-System-Mobile-Phone_60256958833.html?spm=a2700.7724838.0.0.cW9yUR.

[190] Nigeria New Security System Mobile Phone Catcher IMEI and IMSI, Alibaba, https://www.alibaba.com/product-detail/Nigeria-New-Security-System-Mobile-Phone_60256958833.html?spm=a2700.7724838.0.0.cW9yUR.

[191] *Hearing on Examining Law Enforcement Use of Cell Phone Tracking Devices* Before the H. Comm. on Oversight and Gov't Reform, Subcomm. on Info. Tech., 114th Cong. 69 (2015) (Response of Elana Tyrangiel, Principal Deputy Assistant Att'y Gen. of the United States Response 6 to Questions for the Record) (Copy on file with the Committee).

[192] *Hearing on Examining Law Enforcement Use of Cell Phone Tracking Devices* Before the H. Comm. on Oversight and Gov't Reform, Subcomm. on Info. Tech., 114th Cong. 69 (2015) (Responses to Questions for the Record Submitted to Seth Stodder, Assistant Sec'y, Threat Prevention and Sec. Policy, U.S. Dep't of Homeland Sec., by Hon. Jason Chaffetz, Chairman, H. Comm. on Oversight and Gov't Reform (May 25, 2016).

[193] 18 U.S.C. §§ 2510-2522.

with exceptions for law enforcement and service providers. Violations of the Pen Register Statute can be punished by fines or imprisonment for not more than one year, or both.[194]

The Communications Act directs the Federal Communications Commission to "maintain the control for the United States over all the channels of radio transmission" and prohibits the sale of devices that do not comport with FCC standards or the Communications Act.[195] Relevant portions of the Communications Act provide that no person may operate a device similar to an IMSI catcher without a license,[196] no person may manufacture or sell such devices,[197] and no person may interfere with any radio communications.[198] Penalties for violating the Communications Act can include fines (up to $1,600 per violation per day) and criminal penalties including imprisonment for up to a year for a first offense and two years for a second offense.[199]

CONCLUSION

Emerging surveillance technologies like cell-site simulators represent a valuable law enforcement tool, but their domestic use has obvious and serious implications for citizens' Constitutional rights. To ensure that the use of cell-site simulators and other similar tools does not infringe on the rights guaranteed in the Constitution, the use should be limited, and a high degree of transparency is critical. Furthermore, there must be a universal and well-understood standard by which these technologies are deployed.

Congress is best positioned to ensure that appropriate safeguards are put in place. As Justices Alito, Ginsburg, Breyer, and Kagan pointed out in a concurring opinion in *Jones*:

> In circumstances involving dramatic technological change, the best solution to privacy concerns may be legislative. A legislative body is well situated to gauge changing public attitudes, to draw detailed lines, and to balance privacy and public safety in a comprehensive way.[200]

---

[194] 18 U.S.C. §3121(d).

[195] 47 U.S.C. § 302a (b).

[196] 47 U.S.C. § 301 ("No person shall use or operate any apparatus for the transmission of energy or communications or signals by radio...except under and in accordance with [the Communications] Act and with a license in that behalf granted under the provisions of this Act.").

[197] 47 U.S.C. § 302a(b) ("No person shall manufacture, import, sell, offer for sale, or ship devices or home electronic equipment and systems, or use devices, which fail to comply with regulations promulgated pursuant to this section.").

[198] 47 U.S.C. § 333 ("No person shall willfully or maliciously interfere with or cause interference to any radio communications of any station licensed or authorized by or under [the Communications] Act or operated by the United States Government.").

[199] 47 U.S.C. §§ 401, 501, 503, 510; 47 C.F.R. § 1.80(b) (3) (2016).

[200] U.S. v. Jones, 565 U.S. 429-30 (2012) (Alito, J. concurring).

Congress should establish a legal framework that governs government agencies, commercial entities, and private citizens' access to and use of geolocation data, including geolocation data obtained by the use of a cell-site simulator.

Congress should pass legislation to establish a clear, nationwide framework for when and how geolocation information can be accessed and used.

In the meantime:

a. DOJ and DHS should make federal funding and/or approval of cell-site simulator technology to state and local law enforcement contingent on a requirement that these law enforcement agencies at a minimum adopt the new and enhanced guidelines that have been promulgated by DOJ and DHS for the use of these devices.

b. Non-disclosure agreements should be replaced with agreements that require clarity and candor to the court whenever a cell-site simulator has been used by law enforcement in a criminal investigation.

c. State and local law enforcement agencies should at a minimum adopt policies for the use of cell-site simulators that are equivalent to the new and enhanced guidelines DOJ and DHS have established for their use of these devices.

d. All law enforcement agencies at all levels should be candid with the courts on their use of cell-site simulator devices.

e. In light of TIGTA's reported non-use of its cell-site simulator technology since its initial purchase in 2008, the agency should strongly consider decommissioning the device.

f. Individual states should enact legislation that governs how law enforcement uses cell-site simulation technology. Legislation should require, with limited exceptions, issuance of a probable cause based warrant prior to law enforcement's use of these devices.

www.ingramcontent.com/pod-product-compliance
Lightning Source LLC
Chambersburg PA
CBHW081540280526
45788CB00010B/3308